Brain Garden

By Aaron Fields

Published by The Write Perspective, LLC

ISBN: 978-1-953962-99-7

Inside you is a wonderful, growing world — a Brain Garden full of thoughts, feelings, and amazing ideas.
Some days your garden feels sunny.
Some days it feels stormy.
Some days it feels a little messy.
And that's okay.

This book will help you understand your garden, care for it, and learn the tools that help it grow.
You are the gardener — and your garden is becoming something beautiful.

Every child has a Brain Garden — a special place inside where thoughts, feelings, and ideas grow.

Some seeds grow into calm thoughts. Some grow into big feelings. Some grow into brave choices and kind actions.

CALM
BRAVE
CHOICES
KIND
ACTIONS

Your Brain Garden starts with tiny seeds you're born with. Every day, it grows a little more — just like you.

In your garden, there is a Feelings Patch. This is where feelings pop up like flowers. Some are gentle… some grow fast… and some feel prickly.

There is also a Thinking Tree.
It helps you plan, decide, and understand the world. It grows slowly, branch by branch.

CHOICES PLANS

IDEAS

QUESTIONS

And in the middle of your Brain Garden lives your Calm Center —a soft, steady place inside you that helps your thoughts and feelings work together.

Sometimes your Feelings Patch grows super fast. Big feelings burst out like wild vines —anger, sadness, excitement, or worry.

When big feelings spread everywhere, your garden might feel messy or tangled. That's okay — gardens get messy sometimes.

Your Calm Center is like the gardener inside you. When things get tangled, the gardener steps in to help.

The gardener takes deep breaths… slows down…and looks around to see what the garden needs.

Sometimes the garden needs water — like a drink, a rest, or a snack.

Sometimes it needs sunshine —
kind words, a hug, or a quiet moment
with someone you love.

And sometimes the gardener needs help from a grown-up who can sit nearby, listen, and remind you that you're safe.

When your Calm Center gets the help it needs, your Feelings Patch settles down. The wild vines loosen…

...and your Thinking Tree can grow again.
Tall.
Strong.
Steady.

Every time you practice calming your garden, your gardener becomes wiser and braver.

You learn which tools help:
breathing…
talking…
drawing…
hugging…
moving your body…
or just taking a break.

And little by little,
your Brain Garden grows into a place
full of:
kindness,
courage,
curiosity,
and calm.

Your Brain Garden doesn't have to be perfect. It just needs care — and you already have everything you need to take care of it.

So take a deep breath, little gardener.
Your brain is growing every day.
And your garden…
is becoming something beautiful.

Notes for Grown-Ups & Therapists

Understanding the Brain Garden Metaphor

The Brain Garden uses a gentle, child-friendly metaphor to help children understand their emotions, behaviors, and inner world. This story can be used by parents, caregivers, teachers, and therapists to support emotional regulation, resilience, and communication.

🌼 The Garden Metaphor Explained

The metaphor helps children visualize their internal experiences in non-threatening ways.

1. The Feelings Patch

Represents the emotional center of the brain.
Just like flowers, feelings:

- Come in many types
- Grow quickly
- Need different kinds of care
- Can be overwhelming if left untended

Children learn that *all feelings are allowed, and all feelings can be cared for.*

---

2. The Thinking Tree

Represents the developing prefrontal cortex — the part of the brain responsible for:

- planning
- problem-solving
- decision-making
- impulse control

When emotions flood the system, the Thinking Tree can't "grow."
This teaches children that calming the garden helps them think more clearly.

---

3. The Calm Center / Gardener

Represents the child's growing ability to self-regulate.
The "gardener" observes feelings without judgment and helps bring balance back to the garden.

This reflects real-life emotional regulation skills such as:

- deep breathing
- pausing
- asking for help
- using calming tools
- expressing needs

Emotional Regulation (for Adults)

Emotional regulation is the ability to recognize, understand, and manage emotions in healthy ways. Children are not born with this skill — they borrow regulation from the adults who care for them.

Healthy regulation develops through:

- predictable routines
- warm caregiving
- modeling calm behavior
- having emotions named and validated
- practicing calming tools with a safe adult

Children learn not by explanation alone, but through repeated experience.

Co-Regulation (for Adults & Therapists)

Co-regulation is the process of helping a child regulate by sharing your calm presence.

Co-regulation looks like:

- sitting near a child during big feelings
- using a soft voice
- offering a hug or physical reassurance
- slowing your own breathing
- validating their experience ("This is hard. I'm here.")

Co-regulation teaches the brain:

"I am safe. I can calm down. I am not alone."

This is the foundation for self-regulation in adulthood.

How to Use This Book Therapeutically

At home:

- Read the book during calm moments.
- Ask, "What's growing in your garden today?"
- Use garden language during emotional moments.
- Encourage your child to name the "weather" or "plants" inside.

In therapy or SEL sessions:

- Use a whiteboard or paper to draw the child's Brain Garden.
- Identify "feeling flowers," "weeds," and "calming tools."
- Practice breathing as the "gardener taking care of the plants."

In classrooms:

- Use the garden language for morning check-ins.
- Create a "Calm Center" space.
- Teach students their emotional tools as "garden tools."

For parents:

- The garden metaphor reduces shame and increases curiosity.
- Allows children to talk about inner experiences safely.
- Strengthens emotional literacy, empathy, and problem-solving.

Every child has a Brain Garden — a magical place where thoughts, feelings, and ideas grow.

Some feelings bloom like bright flowers. Some grow fast like wild vines. Some days the garden feels calm… and some days it feels tangled.

The Brain Garden is a warm, empowering story that helps children understand their inner world with curiosity instead of fear. Through gentle metaphors and soothing illustrations, kids learn how to:

- recognize their feelings
- calm their bodies
- use coping tools
- ask for help
- grow confidence, kindness, and resilience

Perfect for parents, therapists, teachers, and caregivers, this book turns emotional regulation into something visual, simple, and nurturing — a garden every child can learn to care for.

www.ingramcontent.com/pod-product-compliance
Lightning Source LLC
LaVergne TN
LVHW060642110826
845147LV00018B/1027

* 9 7 8 1 9 5 3 9 6 2 9 9 7 *